E   V   E

R   *Y*   *O*

N *E* **H**

OCTOPUS BOOKS

E

R

E

PORTLAND   DENVER   OMAHA

CECILY IDDINGS

EVERYONE HERE

EVERYONE HERE

BY CECILY IDDINGS

COPYRIGHT © 2014

ALL RIGHTS RESERVED

PUBLISHED BY OCTOPUS BOOKS

WWW.OCTOPUSBOOKS.NET

DISTRIBUTED BY SMALL PRESS DISTRIBUTION

WWW.SPDBOOKS.ORG

ISBN 978-0-9851182-8-0 [PBK]

BOOK DESIGN BY DREW SCOTT SWENHAUGEN

ONE

LYMAN STREET 1

REALLY TALKING 3

MY MAGIC MOUNTAIN 5

AMERICAN SINGER CANARY 8

THINGS WE DON'T LIKE THAT WE DON'T LIKE 10

YOUR HOUSE IS MY HOUSE 12

LONG-TERM COMPANION 14

HARD SCRABBLE 16

COME TRUST ME 18

EASY GO 20

A CONCENTRATION PROBLEM 21

SWEET UM 23

NIGHTS 25

TWO

LIKED IT 29

THREE

WHY NOT STAY IN THE KITCHEN 55

SPONTANEOUSLY 57

FACTS ON FILE 59

MY MARTIAL ARTS 61

SNAKE EATS PREGNANT EWE 63

OUR INTEREST ACCRUES INTEREST 64

PET DISASTROUS 66

MY WAITING ROOM 68

FACTS OF LIFE 70

LIVING ROOM 71

I AM SO GREAT 73

TOWN ROAD ENDS HERE HOWEVER 75

PARTS OF CLASSICS 77

TEETHING RING 79

FOUR

THE DECISION TREE 83

ACKNOWLEDGMENTS

No one

there. Everyone

here.

ROBERT   CREELEY

ONE

LYMAN STREET

I relapse
in that draft where the door
was once. A machine

removed most of the street
then filled it in again.
We say it's the same

but it's not at all. Now the walls
vibrate. The farmer
barely sleeps,

my pictures hesitate, the latches
want unhooking. Next door
someone's irate brothers slash

someone's boyfriend's tires.
The farmer says he won't
be back again

and won't bring beets
when he doesn't come. Fine,
I know, there're other ways to be

bloody-handed and
in the margins where rodents
are dead, a muskrat,

an ordinary rat. What
I'm humming is this: bad
judgment, hunger, sadness?

Merely clumsy, me,
I hit the brakes, I save
a skunk. Later at my stoop

the machine is folded-up
and huger than a hundred of us
in a crowd, put together.

REALLY TALKING

A popular idea in the gallery
was falling upward

above cheese plates and carafes
until basically it escaped

me why I hated to drop down
back first into the arms of the group

when at camp or school
we were goaded into games of confidence

which seemed then
like fifty-two pick-up or a cup trick

like why are you hitting yourself?
why are you hitting yourself?

why are you hitting yourself?
though a mass is nice too, as when

termites from a kicked pile

make sense running or when we demand

fans of the world, rise up!

raise your hands

after your neighbor's hands

then return to your seats

in the stadiums of Providence,

of L.A., Austin, Macon,

of Portland and Green Bay,

where something new is in the air, where

together, friends and enemies,

we are setting a trend.

MY MAGIC MOUNTAIN

I am coming down
when I finish
this trouble I am
troubled by making.
Or is that doubt
talking in a voice
like ice breaking.
It's not disappearing
it's conjuring
more water.
The patients
have patience,
making wills, missing
the old well days
in the flatlands
where I for example
carried a messenger
bag though rarely
a message.

We dandle

our consumption.

We're supposed

to get better

but it's better

to stay sick.

Though bored

of my gadget

and blue dinners

and seeing the screen

saved I log in

I slog on I plug

my ears I pick

a password

no one can guess:

I would like

a better reason

to think.

Is anyone made over

when the makeover

is made? You

can have a treatment and

a treat too and the view
is always changing
and there's always
something new.
In her carriage
the baby rubs bald
the back of her head
with turning to see.

AMERICAN SINGER CANARY

I tired of trying
to learn the language
no one spoke to me.
For the survival
of my species
I cultivated a tilt
of inquisition
and I burbled and hopped,
which was sufficient
for buying, for instance,
worsted wool blazers
and personal pizzas,
or for saying,
The cage is roomy but
the rent is too high.
I could communicate
with my pupils in
neat little rows:
B plus, A minus, C, C...

I imagined them
wearing plaid or
matching jackets
and choosing on casual days
from a list of outfits
administrators approved.
I thought of them thinking.
I thought we were at war
all dressed in slogans and logos,
like a series of easy readers
about the good-girl triplets
Flicka, Ricka, and Dicka,
who rescue a kitten
and look very much alike.
The blackboard said,
There's an error
in this sentence.
I spotted it immediately
and it couldn't fix.

THINGS WE DON'T LIKE THAT WE DON'T LIKE

No one there
and everyone here
dying to make me
room, in which in dying
they left a lot undone.
Whereof I do not know
thereof I can't be curious:
why does it adhere
as much to the idea
as the shopping guide?
Everyone continues to prefer
the image of a person
above all else, whether
handsome or grotesque
or a queen addressing you
that is the artist.
We like gossip.
A rumor makes me
wonder. I want to do

everyone, but no one

there, no one there, no

one here. Here I must be

a house you knock on

that only knocks back.

Difficult to know

if anyone is ever at home.

I want to do everything

I don't understand. Coming

inside I read a sentence

aspiring to do

a little thing, putting dust

in the corner, paint

on the floor, move around

the modifiers.

The sentence offered a little room.

Yes, it said, it matters

what you say about me

like it matters what I like

when I try to like.

YOUR HOUSE IS MY HOUSE

It was easy to get into.

Someone had been there before and knew the tune.

There you had a hotel for a song

and a boy bringing

drinks to you and no other

guests. It was easy to get into

when I applied myself, someone who made

the grade, someone well

checked. Let go

the string, lift the kite

my kite coach said.

In the background unchecked

men and women

grew flowers showy

sold bananas almost free

for some reason.

A winning smile kicked a winning kick.

The crowd went wild

with a clap-clap, stomp-stomp

it was easy to get into.

We were so far from the race

at every revolution

of the fast cars only a baby

would cry at the terrible sound

like a hundred trains on a hundred tracks

like the baby's baby screaming and uncomfortable

in the future like no one would come.

There

from the open windows

in the private rooms the kite

meant to celebrate

an easy reach into

blue blue sky

but engineered on lines in the wind

always a dictator in the works.

LONG-TERM COMPANION

To forestall loneliness
I have had God
installed permanently
in my soul like an iPod
with a never-ending
battery and an all-prayer
playlist or like
a big daddy
or a wiretap
and I am certain
I am better
off. Unlike Emerson
I won't want
to visit my love
who has died and won't
open the coffin
and won't come out
shaken calm
won't forever change

myself or the rhetoric

of a new empire where

in a depression

filled with farmland

my mother leans

against a pitchfork

and looks as if to say

with so much work here

who needs comfort?

HARD SCRABBLE

It's required that I mention
the clit. Er, but look, the view!
From the ice-cap, done in oils,
isn't that easier to talk about,
or consider the spelling of qi,
which one finds emanating
out of certain parts,
like my heart,
my sexy heart.
Those wags jeered
onward ho! all the way home.
They were pugs.
Not like you, darling, smiting
the wine, shining the train,
toeing the line, headed
toward Oz or wherever
it is you go.
The boat's sheen of pitch means it's yar.
The emblem of the fox

and dove means abide
or be clever. The critics are gone
so I gin you in the elms
with resin inside
and blurry leaves outside.
The crag-bound sheep
dolloped into place and gooey
above the several bays
and below the mountain-top
are naïf naïf not faux naïf.
This is altogether a little ad for me
and for you, my enabler,
for the way we can't move
up or down, it's fabulous,
uncomfortable, we're on.

COME TRUST ME

You'll get used
to it. You'll say
I know what's up, hell
yeah, like cross-dressing
or separating green glass
from clear, I'm more
expert today than yesterday.
Why are zombies
better scream-getters
than the Blob is,
I agree, a question
only sort of
going nowhere new,
even for a deep thinker
like me, and the living
room will overfill
when they come home.
I can go home
too where the couch is comfy

and knick-knacks appear in

normal order

mostly, though stranger

after the streets asunder

to which I become

accustomed.

I am trying

and trying not to surprise you.

I am promising

the closed lily

you squeamishly regard

puffy as a drowned finger

will open soon

and be okay

until liver spots

develop and parts

start to fall.

EASY GO

Fundamentally it's hard to trust
the library when it loses bricks
from its fifteenth story,

and I don't trust my mentor
either who never recommended me
to the institute for better

or worse. For so many so-so years
I kept a house full of chickens
with a doubtful disease,

I kept a lousy prognosticator,
we kept all our eyes stacked
like masonry on each other.

Nearby we're afraid of nearly
everything, of you
if you catch my drift.

A CONCENTRATION PROBLEM

I long

to know heuristically

my anchor said

so she reported

daily

first noting the cold front

beyond the fence

then investigating the optical illusion

of waves or concentric rings

caused by the narrowness

of the pickets.

Soon she collected

owl pellets

the producer prised

open almost with a gaze

with spectacular glances.

In dark glasses at a protest

she interviewed an escapee

asking did he cry before flight

and when the break

in the chain link appeared

who did he call

and who came?

My anchor wanted children.

My producer an expert administrator

stopped the tape

and rewound to

I think every minute

every day I am

lucky

which the escapee

had lowered his voice

and looked grateful to say.

He became a special feature,

a clip to play on holidays.

The anchor's a bare arm

and microphone.

The producer's cut out

the dull bits and I am the edge

of his edits.

SWEET UM

Hopefully the ice cream
will amaze you!
—though someone who knows
tells me what I mean:

I hope I amaze you.
So I've bought a straw hat,
the first warm one of its kind,
and on its brim Jack and Jill
and up top the well
and underneath fur
for all winter long.

Seriously, kidding.
That's a lot like me.

Here's my swiss army watch,
square-faced, telling
three times. Here's a story

on accident, oops, sorry.

Here I am poorly juggling

two chocolates and a lollipop,

loops first, pell-mell last.

It's a talent I have,

the leaves turning

quickly golder, are you

looking?

NIGHTS

I do

if you'll tell me

in stories like a mantis

leashed to a bed

where it's kill

or be killed at home

with a cupboard and knives.

The cupboard kills the knife.

The knife smothers the cupboard.

Once you find the knothole

you keep watching the show

keep going. You know

the killer by being

alive. The winner tells

the story you know

by heart when at bedtime

it can't sleep

can't part.

TWO

LIKED IT

It's the lifted skirt of the dervish

Like a top wobbling but not

Winding down it's the mistake

My mother's dead

Boyfriend rests on the air

Dead pilgrims eat my heart

I put on a dress everyone

I love signs

And strangers sign it too

Dead before I even glittered

In anyone's eyes he can't

Know what's being buried

We put it inside me

Dear every father I fuck

This time when you lose it

You lose it to me

One therapist after another climbs

Through the silver ceiling

We put them inside me where

My greenest is and growing

A little wound until it tore

I couldn't close up

The loudest voice in the room

The therapists were twin

Babies from heaven

Their wings beat in my mouth

Drier dustier faltering

Just go home they said

Just let's set some rules

Let's count our blessings

My fillings buzzing

My holes agape no no

Certainly no going home

Dear doctors no home

She said should I call the police

My lover slapped me and left

To smoke it's debatable

I won't debate it

Girls were all around

Holding my hands brushing me

Me a pony and ribboned

It didn't even hurt! I cleared

That low wall in the far field

A man danced his skirts rose

I grew older and older

She kissed my cheek you know

You owe at least that

A woman asleep all afternoon

Or pissy picking tinsel off the rug

Climbed the ladder separately

Silver settler footprints

Leaving going gone it's a pity

Those couples who die off

Together what's the glittering

Prize what new land's there

I rub between husband and wife

As pixels do I remember

I was left out of the frame

They needed a view not more wall

I put the scary book in the hall

Then of course the hall turns

Horrible too my love's not

The contaminated evidence

But it ruins what I want

To know with what I don't

You will not be left alone

It was a meeting of vast tissue usage

A horror show under the bandage

Should I call the police she asked

My finger went in knuckle-deep

The nubbin down there gory

Rubbed it until he said

It hurts it's not enough bring me

And I said I cannot on the ferry

Upon which we all fell to crying

Drying our tears on our skirts

And I wanted my mother

And I took back my hand

We put it inside me

Bloody the finest

The loudest

Little soaps in crinkle paper

And little bottles and neat folds

Just for us in our pilgrim room

In new sheets the alarm

Slapping us awake shyly

Down into the street strangers

In pajamas new from dreaming

You were ignoring me like

I hadn't been there all along

Though I felt solid I felt to

Exist I was burying a melon

With my hand then emergency's

Over they said all's well

How safe who's alone

A bag a towel one name-tag

A wound on the bed you

Were gone gone

I cannot on the ferry dance like

Her but I open my legs and

Scissor you on this last day

Before the last day

My mother's dead boyfriend

Tattooed on your shoulders

The island a prison the explorers

Stinking with scurvy she's owed

A life she can't collect

I slink into your rotten arms

Your loved tattoo put my

Hands in the wound and

Daddy the hole

You will not be left alone

A greeter will give you a name-tag

The officer is kind

The doctor much too young

We feel he is fake sneaking

Around raping patients

Something wrong in any case

Too young and one question is

What about the self-castration

What can we do for

The dead pilgrims who respond

Ascetically even to antidepressants

Should I call the police

Are they bored

On the threshold hesitating

One senses either tragedy

Or striptease might be next

These men are hard

These men have real bullets

The hallway carpet is a nice

Place to stop drinking

Potluck a feast

Even therapists might help

Themselves Indians and

Cowboys Cops and Robbers

Beautiful Wife and

Generous Friend we

Can't leave ourselves alone

We will sing the song of our

Self petting the nap flat

Our name-tagged Self

Our Loudest Voice our

Love fucking us together

I don't care about the sofa

I want a fucking home

I want three loved houses all

At once my father

Wants a dog of the right size

And to poison the rats

Digging bodies on the esplanade

One therapist after another drives

Late at night skirting the fear

Of having one leg severed as you

Enter or exit the car or crosswalk

A problem that dates back to how

She slept while her lover died

When it happens that way well

We wake up on our own

Two men punch each other

On stage after bourbons

Improvisationally an apology

For drinking too much for

Our pleasure she sends her love

He makes my joke a cartoon

With the loudest voice in the room

Bring me your finest finest finery

Bring me a Coke

You will not be left alone

Even if you are well a man

At the market says oh hothouse

Tomatoes and dismisses them

Red yes but he says just

No good inside

My mother's dead boyfriend left

For me a ribbed red shirt

And a blue star he falls

Asleep heavy on top

And that's me! Under there!

The loudest voice in the room!

We put it inside me

Shaped perfectly opposite

Moving at the finest volume

Please please please

I am pro-coincidence I analogize

These strangers don't know you

Only remember it like a dream

It was like fucking a loved

Couch burying the therapists

All named the same and trying

To dig out from inside me

Me an elephant who swallows

Whole families one child after another

Pilgrims upon pilgrims nobody dies

In here nobody escapes until away

So long they grow a new

Nation of their last voice

A whole half a language

Unlike you now

I'll tell you about my wife

An eye doctor and my children

Still rather pet-like and the city

A clam— an oyster—

Oh fuck it who cares

Everyone who gets on this bus

Has the same damn idea

It's better than the movie

But unrepeatable and without

Guarantees vibes chemistry etc.

She sweetly compares

The cock to a flower then

This cock to another cock

And so goes the course of true

Love etc. I've had exactly one

Mistake in digging it out

Failing to account for the sand

If I am honest in unburying

My monstrosity I've choked

My wife unfortunately

These are the choices

We make in general

I am appalled but this

Action must continue

Unless as my mother says

The only thing I must do is

Take her last breath

Only your voice counts

Only the body wounds

Only what I won't ask

To settle in like pilgrims

Tilled medicinal in soil

Know how easily I fall

In there how easy out

Maybe electrodes make me

Write it twitching

Only your strangled voice

Only the skirt's lift and dash

I feel lifted want to stay

Wish I'd stay

My mom's dead boyfriend

Gets in among the clothes

Her skirt's hiked up sexy

He smells like mud this trail's

A mess of poison ivy

He holds my hand and dies

Of love says now she'll

Never know more about me

Now I'm gone you're going

I haven't seen the sky

In days bring me home

Some young ones I'll marry

The girls I'll bend over the boys

Under the guide stars

In this hospital this emergency

And all the next

I planned to stay on the futon

Worried by all the crap you hung

Vitrines and brown smears

Collages glued with toothpaste

A ship of unkind pilgrims

On the way to prison

Walls that don't trap spy

We will not be left alone

With shoelaces shaving

Make of me a mirrored ceiling

To watch through it the record

Of our new worlds

Mine yours yours mine

When I left I was gone

Like butter clarified thicker

Sweeter sex knuckles calloused

You don't know your own

Strength spent this holiday

Slipping handfuls of debt

Into my newest body holes

You owe me you after

All who knows now where

To find those years but me

Who was weirdly constant

As a ghost ship a lost colony

A satellite powered off

Orbiting darkly

He waited his wounds

Open on the open road

You will not be left alone

It isn't fair beaten into us

He puts his dead arms

On the far-off glitter of me

My mother sews a suit

In a locked room sun shining

Something I owe you she says

He says I am in love with this

Life I am in love

I love this life I love love

It's your story it goes

Wrong you will not be left

Alone I can't leave it alone

Advised it's a fear of being

Halved I feel lifted

I bobble at level neither

Too happy nor too sad both

Balanced and dull doctors tend

Our wounds the finest

Voice must be yours under

This heavy skirt rising

In the new world dust from

Which we will go on no

Further though still our spirits

Spin on that point too

I made no mistake

That first night I refused

My new home instead mushed

Myself against the fins

Cut my arms in the sea

Stung alight with night

Animals each stroke repeated

Rippled found the seahorse's

Pocket where the room

Tiny was built for me

Making the bed just so

Bringing the man just close

Enough to talk don't stop

Keep going please go

Some day I might die

You might not be left alone

She can't quite trust that to

Mend the wounds when the police

Gather at the ending

Of a stranger whose emergency

Who says this is not my beautiful

Life cuffed to my perfect doubt why

Trust him who would not

Lead us out together

THREE

WHY NOT STAY IN THE KITCHEN

Because what do I do
there but cook eat talk.
Because I do not like
ovens and knives but find
the party punishing.
For me unnatural heat
for the guests soufflé
or would they rather rabbit.
I can't find rabbit
though nearby legions
nibble tremble fuck.
Nothing for the mob
rampaging the bathroom
to damage a dear
soap dish to yank
the shower curtains
that clicked reassuringly close
and open on something like
ball bearings. Why not

bury the hatchet

asks a deviled egg. Why

when the guests advance

like a cell of sleepers

who look like me

or you and mean

nothing personal

why when they seize

the kitchen where

the frequency

of home accidents turns

the ladyfingers grim

why do I arrange

crackers and why

touch each one?

SPONTANEOUSLY

To the vegetable aisle one excellent poet
after another files! Though they like me

mistrust the supermarket more and more.
Someone's miserable about this radish.
There are free radicals in the tomatoes,

the potatoes are basically flab. At the fancy store

entirely of my own accord I bought
the fire-roasted frozen corn
though it cost a dollar more.
As some kernels were blackened
on the package I thought

my that looks good.

People call them niblets. I don't know myself
why, when the advertisement

says this produce, that product

has a brand new surprise, I forget to suspect

it isn't a prize.

FACTS ON FILE

I could've been a contender I mean

I should've probably invested in real

Estate by this late date

Nobody gave me a superlative

My friend got the wrong one

He got grumpy and you'd've unliked

Yours too isn't it nice

To spend some hours wondering why

You don't all laugh more

At my jokes since I'm funny ha

Ha though strangely hard to train

Failing for example to appreciate

The tyger tyger for far far longer

Than I should've and still fuzzy

Even on the Number One Painter of Light

Despite having an imperialist's grasp

Of story this voice of mine offends

Me awfully some nights I dance

To the beat of the unkinder parent

But better thought sobbed seeing

It's true I'm buried too

By happy days

MY MARTIAL ARTS

After the refereed fights
if I won I believed
something extra
as if in the dark
I found the clock
and TV and remote
by heaven
sent. I asked
my hand what it felt
and it told me before I knew
the car hood under frost
or father's mustache
I should not touch.
Like the sing-song
bubbles from aquariums
in the house next door
my hand was far away
soothing. I asked it
were we sundry.

I asked who
pulled the punches
and who knew first
which ones landed badly
and what was good.

SNAKE EATS PREGNANT EWE

About one's flab it is one's own.

What's mine is mine and moves with me

so long as I can move

in my ever-enormouser dresses

in trucks that almost breathing work up the road

from gear to gear, mouse house to

tony nook. What could live

in my huge mind I don't already know,

I haven't met, I do not

repeat. What might be with me

under the warm bath, the familiar soap.

About one's baby out he goes

and goes. About his reasons.

About my skin I am my skin

but I am not my liver.

Some things pass through

completely untouching.

I am the benefits supervisor.

The system is as strange to me as me

still I give it work

and it works in me.

63

OUR INTEREST ACCRUES INTEREST

All my false friends come
over and party.
Meryl suggests strip
poker instead we talk
of money. Barry's portfolio
is inexhaustible,
Barry inexorable,
Barry. No one's natural
resource. After the gold
standard standards
tended toward
abstraction. I care
for my real friends
so greatly I can't
bear them.
There's just a store
of misunder
standing in for me.
I imagine them

the conversations

I shy from

when I gain you.

But for everything else

I have credit.

We love olives

and olives are rich,

Sara reminds us

of the Third World.

Where we could be

millionaires, uneasy perhaps

but easier than most.

Meryl on the roof

overlooks the slum

the oligarchy overlooks.

Overnight pennies slap

into our laps automatic

as the moon.

They smell of old

wounds. They hurt

the tender more.

PET DISASTROUS

That intention I had
I failed to protect.

It drank the bad water
and bloated.

It got beat up.
A Subaru ran

over it.
An Outback. It cried quieter,
quieter, it stopped.

I was addled inept,
I'd lost the prescription,
so its side effects were missing.
It was normal and quickly worse.

I wrung my hands and moved

onto some final stage, tapped

the microphone, searching the floor

for a cannibal, thinking

dead things are much deader

when you don't eat them.

The doc said do this,

no thanks said the diners,

the coroner said

you didn't, did you.

MY WAITING ROOM

A woman looked at me
directly then I looked
at the fish tank
for what felt like hours.
For what felt like hours
the good soldier left
the stranger shackled
to the ceiling.
For like hours. For like
a night. Felt like what.
It was time to straighten
so I stacked the dishes
for what felt like hours.
When he died he could not
lay himself down. I watched
a good show on TV
for a long time. I felt
each day like an easy
answer. I felt it like

a shopper wanting

what I wanted when

I wanted it. I met

no one's eyes. I felt

I should accept

this present I did

not choose

and can't help

but deserve.

FACTS OF LIFE

Anxious alone I would raise a second

Comer I said bye to my maybe baby

He was of water more than wine

He would've wailed I didn't

When the storm was coming all

The water went first pulled off-shelf

Like waves from the shore

Where the longer they leave the harder

They come

He couldn't miss me nor I him

My voice broke I glued my eyes

To keep it together NO CRYBABIES

They say at the door since sweeties

We are made confectionery

And I forgot becoming

Him into me melts me into you

Coming to I felt helter skelter felt

Unhouseled

LIVING ROOM

In the carpet
is a story, man buys camel,
camel walks, camel walks,
and several geometric proofs.

The door is alarmed!
But the window has a
vacant sign:
upstairs room,
shelf, cabinet, lock,
fair rent.

In the living room,
an armchair where
one child sits,
seriously unappealing,
wanting

to scotchtape over every line

to save every word,

to give itself more glare.

It wonders where

a mother is who isn't anywhere

at home. Who accounts

empty quarters with a calculator

that records amounts

received, withdrawn, printing a list

that goes on, on, on,

that stops, turns a corner,

greets the isosceles

where the poker rests,

shelters the floor, meets the door,

tells the child, well

one thing's sure.

I AM SO GREAT

That the tree that owns itself
is not itself might disappoint you
like it disappointed me.

Its predecessor toppled, sorry to say,
roots rotting, and then Junior Ladies
regrew it with an acorn and care.

Emily Dickinson is not so great,
my father tells me. Better to take vitamins
and sleep enough, Cecily, Emily

Dickinson is no John Donne
and John Donne no Shakespeare,
and who knows really who he was?

The Colonel who truly bore a great love
for the white oak had a great desire
that the oak be self-possessed,

and thus he willed it. With high hopes
one afternoon, Emily and a cousin
no one much remembers

decided to be distinguished. I lived
by that oak. I was more moving
but it had more mastery,

the road narrowing to a single lane
to give it reach. All the vehicles
slowed, everyone that passed

passed with hesitation.

TOWN ROAD ENDS HERE HOWEVER

Though my father's dead I say
at the front,

called away.
The flag's hanged half mast then half
that then half again, until it's time

to burn it for the right reasons.

I explain this
to the convoy and they wave
goodbye, farewell. The canal

has five heights, from too low
to overflowing,

but every one
is passable. I hardly

need the private way,

which is concrete and continues.

All the country, too, we don't

want to touch the ground.

My father warned

us when he was dead

to keep ourselves alive,

therefore I round the sharp

turn unluckily, using brights and a signal.

PARTS OF CLASSICS

All parts of a classic are equally classic.
An insect larvae obviously
won't grow without food,
observes an important entomologist.
I observe that our hero must leave
and preferably ASAP, but not before
he's produced that memorable speech
or fucked his mother.
I like her better. She stays home
and puts out little soldiers
or more mothers. It's pretty
terrible but familiar.
Through a pretty thin page
one part of a classic may be visible
beneath another part, and beneath
one classic may be part of a preceding
classic. In origami originally
you folded straight lines,
but the new institute for folding

tries curves or one cut. Now
a paper beetle seems round
though not exactly real.
The singer was not trained
classically. That's why
her oldie-but-goodie sounds strange.
The classics are partly boring.
The teacher is partly mean.
When we read a good part, I fold
over a corner, you put down a flag.

TEETHING RING

When I asked for a sitter I ended up
with a woman posing first vampish

then impoverished, both ways ignorant
of the baby.

Since then I knew not what to do
what else to do but

mistake the baby
through the cosmorama

to see All the World in a Box.

The boxes are lacquered cherry and bevel-edged.

The baby has a hole in his head I'm told not to poke.

But I'm a tempted kind
of mother, consequently

I worry over his topography.
All the world disappoints
and the baby is indifferent.

Will he speak?

Will he drool into old age?
Into adage, liquor, evil?

The sloping glass lids fit perfectly
above the soda pop labels and the paper dolls, at least

one from each continent, while the baby's eyes
drift like planchettes, meaningful, maybe.

FOUR

THE DECISION TREE

0. SOME ART

Here is a box cutter now make something

Here in quiet should I

Here at the corner pick a block and walk it

Reach a store here have I enough

The rusty purposeless structure

That is a thinking machine

That in no part moves

Is not a problem here

Here is a painting of a flat grid at night

A lacking building city

Here is the house that might be

Here is the mass of house that was

Here is a city like a video game

Here is not the problem

Have I enough to make it

Here a cut to make

Have I enough to make it

A problem here

The purposeless structure

To make it move

Enough to make

To say it here

1.

Say boy breathe out before you

Pull your trigger

Least if it matters if you hit me

Pull it out right

There you aren't hard like that

Only assholes

Hold it sideways or get in all

Close and give way

You're right she won't I don't

Know you shooter

Spraying my made-up face won't

Let them think tears

Or glue or snot so I show off

Lick swallow smile

2.

How nice we chose ourselves

From the basically nobody

Left in the douchey dark past

Last call for al-co-hall

I'm bikram you're burner

Can't quite afford it but we

Want it all summer all day

I dream about sex like lest we

Expire from the tsunami of

Respect slash lust our pheromones

Inspire in him her him her

We better get a fast car

Baby to get out of here fast

Friends on my say so in our best

Sneakers on our way now we're

On our way poem

3.

They cut off either one tit

Or some fingers then you're

In the tribe and get a QR

Code tattooed anywhere

You choose only we can

Read it so we know who

We are I wanna be insider

Than I am you go in a

Locked room to play escape-

From-the-room because

It is fun you wear this hood

And have fun if you don't

Struggle the tube is nice

Going down like coke

Numb numb numb and

You feel cooler for hours

We do this for the love

Of you we do this for you

And your damned wasted

Freeness

4.

I wanna be insider than

I am then I am VIP

And backstage accessing

Choosing my hand on

Your thigh I choose

Higher backer more-er

If I want it too bad too

Bad she renames herself

Rich he's in chambray shorts

And tats we voted for

This beach and its dune

Were built for us to

Bring it to the end of

The world we know

The beginning of the

One we prescripted

As if in punishment

A never quite meaning-

Less pun

5.

Is it angry voice

American girl voice

You capable user

Of your natural resources

Knowing the price of every

Thing and the value of ...

True enough says the bodega

Wall each morning

Educate me says the boy

Each day and fuck you too

If you can't take it you don't

Get it is why *The Birds*

Scares me wanna be

Insider you got to be inside

Put the gun in the song because

The gun is the song when

You flinch in my face you

Gasp past me to the ruins

The horror of my path which

Down I skip you sing

Pluck the petals pink us

The heiress and this

The dominion if only you

Take it

6.

Propose it as a choice and

We choose it you are in

A maze of twisty little

Passages all alike if

A labyrinth is less game

More religion since I move

Insider wiser then out

Changed then he's in a maze

Of twisty little passages

All alike he says fuck you

Means fuck me means we have

A choice when I feel most

Belonging you miss the fun

Meaning she's like what's

The point of this he goes

It just is like a tree just

Is and if it talked you'd

Think it was god talking

Like I am that I am

In a maze of twisty

Little passages all alike all

Alike where she's like yeah

Yeah I too dislike it

ACKNOWLEDGMENTS

THANK YOU to the editors of the following journals, where some of these poems have appeared, sometimes in different forms: *Apartment, Article, Boog City, Horse Less Review, jubilat, Meridian, Octopus, Prelude, Saltgrass, Sixth Finch, Spinning Jenny,* and *Spork Press.*

SPECIAL THANKS TO Sandra Barry of the Elizabeth Bishop House in Great Village, Simeon Berry, Rob Crawford, Frank Guan, Chris Hosea, James Tate, Fritz Ward, Dara Wier, members of the workshops at the University of Georgia and University of Massachusetts Amherst, everyone at Octopus Books, and my family—Hally, Carl, Aaron, Tom.

RECENT TITLES AVAILABLE FROM OCTOPUS BOOKS

PICASSO'S TEARS *Wong May*

SORROW ARROW *Emily Kendal Frey*

SOMEONE ELSE'S WEDDING VOWS *Bianca Stone*

SEXUAL BOAT (SEX BOATS) *James Gendron*

MY DEAD *Amy Lawless*

PORTUGUESE *Brandon Shimoda*

HIDER ROSER *Ben Mirov*

BALLOON POP OUTLAW BLACK *Patricia Lockwood*

DEAR JENNY, WE ARE ALL FIND *Jenny Zhang*

THE BLACK FOREST *Christopher DeWeese*

DATE DUE DEC 2 0 2014

WITHDRAWN